Report Writing

A practical guide to effective
report writing, presented in
report form.

Report Writing

A new practical guide to
effective report writing,
presented in report form.

Gordon R. Wainwright, BA, BEd, MBIM, FRSA

Management Update

First published in Great Britain 1984
Reprinted 1985, 1986, 1987
Second revised edition 1990
Reprinted 1992
Management Update Ltd
99A Underdale Road, Shrewsbury SY2 5EE

British Library Cataloguing in
Publication Data
Wainwright, Gordon
Report Writing
1. Report writing
I. Title
808'.066   HF5719
ISBN 0 946679 02 9 Hardback
ISBN 0 946679 01 0 Paperback

Typeset by G. Donald & Co. Ltd

Cover design by Leo Maggs

Printed and bound in Great Britain by
Biddles Ltd, Guildford and King's Lynn

1: Summary

The quality of business and industrial report writing is often inadequate for the demands made upon it. Now, however, more and more organisations are training personnel in the skills of effective report writing. This guide is intended to help them in this work. You, the report writer, will find its usefulness enhanced if you genuinely wish to improve your own powers of self-expression.

You will find that this guide contains the general principles and techniques which are basic to good report writing. The main ones are:

(i) every report should follow a suitable plan and headings should be used to describe and distinguish each of the sections and sub-sections;

(ii) you should determine as clearly as possible what kind of report is required and the full purpose of the report before you begin the work of preparation;

(iii) you should include in your report only such information as is necessary and relevant to your purpose;

(iv) after writing your report, you should review your work and make any changes necessary to

ensure that it fulfils its purpose, says exactly
what you want it to say, and contains no
ambiguities or inaccuracies;

(v) you should write your report within as short a
period of time as possible, writing the body of
the report first and the summary last.

Three appendices accompany this guide which
expand on or supplement some of the points made.
One of them gives advice and guidance on how to
prepare and deliver oral reports, presentations and
briefings.

There is also a further reading list which
recommends several books of particular usefulness to
the report writer.

Table of Contents

2: Introduction

It is important to have well-written and attractively presented reports in business, industry and public service. Writing good reports is an art which can be learned and this guide explains, in report form, the general principles of effective report writing. As far as is known, it is the only publication available which tries to do this. The report form was chosen so that the techniques outlined could be demonstrated at the same time. For this reason, the guide should provide a useful and permanent source of reference.

The emphasis throughout is on providing practical advice to managers and others who have to write reports as part of their jobs. Those who have had several years' experience of writing reports should find that this guide offers a state of the art picture of current practice. They will be able to select those points which they feel might be useful in the future. The beginner should find that he (or she) is provided with a practical guide which takes him (or her) step by step through the process.

In compiling the guide, most of the major authorities on the subject have been consulted. Individual acknowledgement of a general indebtedness is therefore impossible. Acknowledgement is also due to the hundreds of managers, executives, administrators, engineers, scientists and others who have attended the author's courses. Their critical eyes and constructive suggestions have contributed considerably to what is hoped to be a unique and comprehensive statement. Any remaining errors, inaccuracies or other deficiencies are solely the responsibility of the author.

2.1 Definition

A report is an ordered and logical statement. It uses sectional headings and sub-headings. It gives the facts about a situation or problem. It may also consider the case for and/or against a proposed course of action. It may discuss the likely or actual effects of a decision or course of action. It may describe and evaluate the results of work or research. It may simply record a sequence of events.

A report may offer interpretation of the significance of particular facts. It may draw conclusions and/or make recommendations. It may also contain supporting evidence and illustrative material, usually in appendices. Normally, the report will be prefaced by a brief summary.

2.2 Purpose

A report can have any one, or a combination, of a number of purposes. It may simply seek to inform others about a given problem or situation. It may try to persuade its readers to adopt a particular course of action or to agree with a point of view. It may try to predict what the consequences of optional courses of action might be and leave its readers to decide which one to follow.

Whatever the reasons for which a report is required, you will need to ensure that your own objectives in writing the report match these reasons. If they do not, the report will fail in its purpose.

2.3 Types of Reports

Basically, reports can be either formal or informal. The former are usually longer than the latter and written for readerships which are not known personally to the writer. Examples of formal reports would be feasibility study reports for clients, committee reports in a local authority, accident reports, survey reports, and research reports. Examples of informal reports might be those written routinely for your immediate superior, pro forma, visit reports, and sales reports for internal consumption.

Reports can be about work that has been done or about projected work. If they are the former, they may be interim progress, final progress, or instruction reports. If the latter, they may be analytic or advisory. In each case, they can be preliminary, interim or final reports.

The differences between the various kinds of reports are many. They should all, however, follow a similar basic pattern of organisation of the kind described in this guide. There may be little similarity, though, in the choice of words and the amount of information given in each case.

3: Preparation

Reports are written in five stages, namely:

Stage I   Preparation – the period during which information for the report is collected.

Stage II   Assessment – the period during which the writer decides whether he has everything he needs to plan and write the report.

Stage III Planning – the period during which the information which will go into the report is selected and arranged.

Stage IV   Expression – the period during which the report is written.

Stage V   Review – the period during which the first draft is edited and revised for final typing and submission.

The initial letters of these five stages form the mnemonic PAPER which should help you to remember them and the order in which they occur. This section deals with the first stage and shows you how to complete it satisfactorily.

3.1 Task Checklist

During the preparation stage you will need to:

(i) clarify your terms of reference;
(ii) analyse your readership;
(iii) set objectives which the report will achieve;
(iv) collect information
(v) store information.

3.2 Terms of Reference

Clear terms of reference are essential if you are to write an effective report. They should define the purpose, type, scope and readership. Sometimes you will be given this information by whoever has asked you to write the report. If you are not, you will have to produce your own terms of reference. You can use the checklist in this section as a guide. You may, if you wish to be sure, seek approval from the person(s) who commissioned the report before beginning work.

Once you know why you are writing the report, what type of report it should be, how much of the subject it should cover and who will read it, then, and only then, will you be able to complete the remaining steps in this stage effectively.

Ask yourself:

(i) what are the general aims of the report (for example, to inform, to persuade, to place on record, to provide a basis for action)?
(ii) what is the subject of the report (for example, a visit, an inspection, tests carried out)?
(iii) how much information should go into the report (for example, essential facts only, a comprehensive and detailed analysis, a full factual record, mainly recommendations with

only the necessary supporting evidence)?

(iv) what form of report is required (for example, memo, letter, short informal, long formal)?

(v) what resources do you have at your disposal (for example, finance, secretarial or research assistance, technical equipment)?

(vi) who will read the report? (this is the subject of a further checklist in section 3.3)

(vii) to whom will you submit the final report? (reports may not always be submitted to those who asked for them)

(viii) by when must the report be finished?

To illustrate the use of this checklist, let us suppose that you have to write a short report on your duties at work for a new superior. He has not said any more than, 'Let me have a report on what you do around here.' The terms of reference you draw up for yourself might take this form (the numbers following each statement refer to points from the checklist):

"The report will describe in detail (i) the nature of my duties (ii), giving full details of my current workload, as well as recent achievements and proposed objectives for the immediate future (iii). It will be a short informal report (iv) written with the usual secretarial assistance (v). It will be read only by my immediate superior (vi), to whom it will be submitted (vii) on Friday (viii)."

3.3 Readership Analysis

This is a task which may only have to be completed once if all your reports are submitted to the same person and cover the same subject area. However, it is worth doing every time you find yourself writing for a new readership, or dealing with a new subject. The more precisely you can identify in advance who will read your report, what they know of the subject already and what use they are likely to make of what you tell them, the easier the actual writing will become. You should use the checklist in this section to produce an analysis of the likely readership. You can then refer to it at any time to make sure you are writing for your reader(s) and not merely for yourself. Ask yourself:

(i) who is the primary reader (the person who asked for the report)?
((Note: sometimes there can be more than one primary reader, for example, if a committee asks for a report.)

(ii) what does he/she know about the subject already?

(iii) does he/she have any known opinions about the subject?

(iv) who are the secondary readers (whoever else is likely to read the report)?

(v) do they have any previous knowledge or opinions about the subject?

(vi) what do the readers need to know about the subject? Do the needs of secondary readers differ from those of the primary reader?

(vii) are there any special considerations to be borne in mind (for example, the report is for a chairman who demands reports no longer than a single side of paper, or a technical report which will be read by people without a technical background)?

(viii) what response or reaction is required from readers and to what use will they put the information in the report? Will primary and secondary readers vary in their responses?

(ix) what kind of relationship do you wish to establish between yourself and your readers?

(x) what assumptions about the subject are readers likely to have made? What assumptions have you made? If there are differences between the assumptions you have made and those your readers will have made, will these be important differences?

You should also remember that most adults, without training have only limited reading skills. Some methods of assessing readability will be described in section 7.3 of this report.

To show how a readership analysis is conducted, let us take as an example that you are preparing one on the immediate superior who has asked for a report on your duties. There is no need, as we did in section 3.2, to write it in paragraph form if you do not wish to. You can simply answer the questions of the checklist in this form:

(i) Immediate superior.

(ii) Very little since he has just joined the company. He will, however, already have a general knowledge of the various roles individuals fulfil in organisations.

(iii) Not to my knowledge.

(iv) None.

(v) Not applicable.

(vi) He needs enough detail to understand exactly what I do and to be able to judge whether my duties need changing so that they are more in keeping with the way he wants to run the department. It will be better to give too much information rather than too little.

(vii) He may not have the same specialist background as me, so I shall need to use technical terms with care.

(viii) I want him to understand what I do and encourage me to get on with it. I don't want him to make changes for the sake of making changes, hence the need to give him as much information as possible.

(ix) I want him to have enough trust in me and confidence in my abilities to achieve (viii). My report must speak for me when he is deciding what to do about the department.

(x) He may assume my duties need changing to meet changing circumstances in the organisation. I assume that, by asking me for a report, he would like my views on how my role might develop. I assume he is both testing my ability (by not giving me detailed terms of reference) and giving me the opportunity to show initiative (by asking me for the report in the first place). There need be no conflict between our respective assumptions, if I am right.

3.4 Objectives

Once you have clear terms of reference and a precise picture of whom you are writing for, you are in a better position to set yourself objectives against which you can measure your performance. You can then check at any time during the work on the report to see if you are likely to complete it successfully. You will not know, of course, until after the report has been submitted, whether it really is successful. At least the feedback provided by referring to your objectives will help to increase the chances of success.

Objectives should be stated as clearly, concisely and accurately as possible. They should be stated not as intentions (for example, to investigate failures in equipment and machinery), but as results to be achieved. This means that, if we take again the example of a report on your duties for a new superior, they may be set out like this:

The report will:
  (i) demonstrate how each of the items in my job description is covered by my current activities;
 (ii) highlight recent achievements which I feel are worthy of note;
(iii) contain proposed objectives for my activities for the immediate future;
 (iv) contain 1000-1500 words, with my present job description attached as an appendix;
  (v) be completed in first draft by Wednesday to allow for editing and final typing on Thursday and submission on Friday;
 (vi) be written to be understood by a non-specialist, that is, my immediate superior;
(vii) follow standard short informal report format with summary, introduction, body of the report (using appropriate headings), conclusions and recommendations, and an appendix.

The objectives are thus a refinement and a closer definition of key points from the terms of reference and the readership analysis. The last objective (vii) has been included here for illustration for, although the point has not yet been covered, it should be included in all the reports you write after you have completed your study of this guide (see section 5).

Now that you have terms of reference to work to, a readership analysis to guide you and objectives to achieve, you are ready to begin the main part of the first stage in writing a report. You are ready to begin collecting information.

3.5 Collection of Information

Information can be gathered in many ways. You may do it by interviewing people, by reading or research, by carrying out tests, by observation or by doing some other kind of work. The method chosen will be dictated by the nature of the report that will result. In many of the cases with which we are concerned here, the information collected will be the result of some kind of practical work. Tables of results, graphs, notes made and any other available information will be gathered into your hands as you go along. Much of it will be acquired in what seems at the time to be almost a random fashion. You will amass a quantity of facts, inferences and value judgements which will all need to be sifted to sort the wheat from the chaff. There is no need to worry about that yet, though. Far better, at this stage, to concentrate on collection. Selection is a matter for the next stage.

It is better to collect more information than you think you will use, rather than just enough or less. Reports, and indeed most other kinds of written materials, are easier to write when you are able to choose from more than you need. Refer to your objectives from time to time, as well as your terms of reference and readership analysis, and make sure that you are still on target. Make sure that you cover all the angles.

It is worth remembering the questions that journalists bear in mind when they are researching their reports:
Who?
What?
Where?
When?
How?
Why?

If the information you collect answers these basic questions (or as many of them as are relevant to your report; for example, 'When?' may not be a relevant question if your report has no time implications associated with it), then you are more likely than not to find that you have covered your subject thoroughly.

You may also find it useful to use some of the techniques of information collection used by research workers. Before you begin your own enquiries or activities, check to see if someone else has produced a similar report to the one you are preparing. This is known as a literature search. If your organisation has a library, check with the librarian to see if he or she is able to help with this. Consult technical and specialist publications. Consult other experts in the field who are known to you. Consult other departments in the organisation to see if anyone has produced a similar report from their point of view. If the subject is not one where commercial confidentiality or security is an important factor, consult contacts in other organisations.

Prepare a research design, if this is appropriate. You will need to state the hypothesis which you are going to test, the methods you intend to use to achieve this and how you are going to evaluate your findings.

The precise methods you use for each report will obviously vary. There is no magic formula for the collection of information. You have to use whichever techniques your judgement tells you will be the most productive.

3.6 Notemaking and Storage of Information

Whatever your sources of information are, you will need to make notes. You will also need a system for storing the information you have collected. This is true whether you have used your own observations, reports written by others, documents, publications or interviews.

A simple system of alphabetic shorthand will help with the first problem. Most people devise their own method for making notes, but for those who have not developed one, perhaps because they have never previously felt the need, one can be suggested. It has the mnemonic title of VULCAN formed from the initial letters of the first word in each step, and the principal techniques are these:

Step	Examples	Basis of Step
(a) Vowels are generally omitted (but see later rules).	mngmnt, tchncl, scntfc.	Most of the information about a word is gained from its consonants.
(b) Unnecessary words are omitted.	smpl systm alphbtc shrthnd hlps wrtr.	Most of the information in a sentence is gained from the nouns and

		adjectives (plus key verbs, prepositions, negatives, etc.)
(c) Long words are shortened.	prelim, repercns, suppntry.	The first half of a polysyllabic word is usually more informative than the second half.
(d) Common words are abbreviated.	o for of, f for if, th for the, ϙ for and, s for is, → for to, ♯ for that, t for it.	Approximately 25% of writing consists of these 10 words.
(e) Abbreviations are made of other frequently used words.	nec, spec, freq, info.	It is useful to work out abbreviations for other words you use frequently.
(f) Note form of expression used.	VULCAN syst: (a) Vwls omtd. (b) Unec wds omtd. (c) Lng wds shortd. (d) Cmn wds abbd. (e) Abbs freq usd wds. (f) Nte frm exprn usd.	Language is up to 50% redundant and you can usually omit all but the essentials without losing any of the meaning.

When it comes to storing information, one of the most convenient methods is to use postcards kept in a small box. The cards will hold quite large amounts of information in note form and they make cross-referencing much easier than if you use sheets of paper. The cards, being small, also encourage brevity.

Information gained from interviews or personal observation can be stored on cassette or microcassette tapes. Where the facilities exist, it may even be advantageous to store certain information on videocassettes. If you were, for instance, preparing a report on a training system or on visits to company locations, video recordings might be particularly helpful.

Many offices now contain word processors and the disks used on these are ideal for storing many kinds of written and graphic information. The special advantages of doing this are that information can very easily be extracted for immediate inclusion in the report itself, it can be moved from one part of the report to another to see where it fits best and it can be retained for possible future use in subsequent reports and other documents. Word processors are of such potential benefit to report writers that we shall return to this subject in section 7.6.

3.7 Exercises

So that you can assess how well you are able to put the instructions given in this section into practice, it will be useful to attempt at least one of the following exercises:

 (i) Prepare terms of reference for a short report on a visit to one of your organisation's other locations (if there are no other locations, assume a visit to another organisation's premises).

 (ii) Prepare a readership analysis for a person or a group of people other than your immediate superior.

(iii) Prepare a set of objectives either for a report which is occupying you at work at the moment or for a report which you know you will have to produce in the near future.

(iv) Collect information for a short report on the contribution your organisation makes to the economy of the town/city/county in which it is located (or mainly located, in the case of very large organisations).

3.8 Completion Checklist

At the end of this section you should be able to answer the following questions:

  (i) What are the five stages in writing a report?

 (ii) What should be included in the terms of reference?

(iii) What should be considered when making a readership analysis?

(iv) How do objectives differ from terms of reference?

 (v) What methods can be used to collect information?

(vi) What are the steps in the VULCAN system of personal shorthand?

4: Assessment

After completing the Preparation stage and before proceeding to the Planning stage, it is necessary to take stock. You need to pause and consider whether you have everything you require. Unless you can satisfy yourself on the points raised in this section, you are not ready to proceed.

4.1 Task Checklist

During the assessment stage you will need to:

(i) set aside time for an incubation period;

(ii) check the completeness of your preparation;

(iii) ensure that you are ready in all respects to proceed.

4.2 Incubation Period

An incubation period is an amount of time set aside before, during or after an activity in which the mind is allowed to mull over what is proposed or what has been done before moving on to the next step in the process of completing a task successfully. It can also refer to any break in an activity, even if the task is not being consciously thought about.

There is plenty of evidence, from activities as diverse as doing crosswords and trying to come up with innovative solutions to old problems, that incubation periods are of great help in making sound assessments and in forming conclusions and opinions.

You are recommended to allow for an incubation period at this point in the writing of a report for reasons that will become apparent later in this section. There is every reason, however, to allow for an incubation period between any of the stages in report writing, if time permits.

What exactly do you do during an incubation period? You may think about what you have done, using the task checklist and the completion checklist as guides. You may check through the work of a stage systematically, point by point. You may discuss what you have done with others. You may, indeed, do nothing at all and simply allow unconscious mental processes to result in sudden and unexpected insights. The fact that such insights can and do occur can be demonstrated by thinking of past problem-solving activities, for instance. You may well recall situations when you have been working on a puzzle or problem and have been unable to solve it, yet you have found that when you returned to the activity later (perhaps the following day) you have inexplicably found the solution to the insoluble. These occasions are examples of incubation periods at work.

Incubation periods may last any time from a few minutes to several days or weeks. How long a period it is will depend more on how much time is available than on the activity. As a general rule, however, longer periods are needed for more complex activities or intractable problems.

Incubation periods can work before an activity begins, when very little is known about it, but they work best when there is available to you a body of information or knowledge as well as the task or problem to which it relates. That is why an incubation period is particularly appropriate here between the preparation and planning stages.

4.3 Completeness of Preparation

The main point to consider during this assessment stage is whether or not your preparation is complete. It will be useful to have a checklist to assist you in deciding this:

   (i) Have you consulted all your sources of information?

  (ii) Are any sources you have not been able to consult sufficiently important for you to make one further attempt to consult them?

 (iii) Are your notes sufficiently detailed on each aspect of the subject?

 (iv) Have you checked your preparation against your terms of reference, readership analysis and objectives?

  (v) Does your preparation answer the relevant 'journalists' questions (Who? What? Where? When? How? Why?)?

 (vi) If you have been using a research design, does it still seem to be appropriate?

(vii) Is the information you have collected stored in a suitable form and can you gain access to it easily?

4.4 Readiness to Proceed

It is important not to rush the assessment stage if this can be avoided. Sometimes the pressures of work are such that there may be no time for an assessment stage at all. It is not uncommon for reports to be required 'yesterday' and a report writer placed in this situation should recognise how much this will add to his or her problems.

If you know from experience that whoever asks for your reports will try to rush you if at all possible, prepare for this in advance by insisting on more realistic deadlines. If these cannot be obtained, make sure that you are always further ahead with your report than you appear to be. This should then allow you to insert an assessment stage, even if this is only an overnight pause.

However you achieve it, you have to be satisfied in your own mind that you are ready to proceed before moving on to the planning stage.

4.5 Completion Checklist

At the end of this section you should be able to answer the following questions:
- (i) What is an incubation period?
- (ii) What do you do during an incubation period?
- (iii) What factors determine the lengths of incubation periods?
- (iv) When should incubation periods be used?

5: Planning

If the preparation for the report has been carried out properly and if the assessment shows that you are ready to proceed, planning should present few problems. It is, however, a stage in which great care must be exercised in order to prevent unnecessary difficulties arising when it comes to writing the report. Indeed, if the report is well planned, it will almost write itself. All you will have to do is follow your plan point by point and write up the notes which you have decided to include in the report.

Time spent planning is rarely wasted. It is the stage during which the report finally takes shape and you can really begin to see what the end product will look like. The more detailed the plan is, the more clearly you will be able to see exactly what kind of document you will have for your readers.

5.1 Task Checklist

During the planning stage you will need to:

(i) make the final decision on the type of report you will write;

(ii) select the information which you will put in the report;

(iii) plan the arrangement of the selected information within the report;

(iv) pay particular attention to organising the body of the report, using appropriate section headings;

(v) complete all the pre-writing stages in the production of a report.

5.2 Type of Report

The first step you must take when planning is to make a final decision on the type of report you will write. In most cases, this will already have been decided by your terms of reference and your objectives. It is possible, though, that you may have changed your mind during the collection of information. You may have expected to find a great deal of information and in fact have found only a limited amount. This might cause a long, formal report to be replaced by a short, informal report. Then again, the reverse might have happened and you might now be able to write a much more detailed report than you originally envisaged.

Whatever you decide, it will be unwise to change the type of report you are going to write after this point. If you do, the result may be to confuse your readers. It is better to make a final decision now. It will affect the next step and all the others still to follow.

5.3 Selection of Information

If we can assume, then, that you have all the material to hand that you are likely to need, you must now begin the process of sifting through it and selecting the information you will actually use. Rarely will you find that all the material you have acquired is needed. Anything that is not directly relevant to the subject must be discarded. Nothing should be retained without good reason. There is no point in keeping something in the report simply because you have gone to a great deal of trouble to find it out. This is a major temptation the report writer must resist.

If we take an example of the selection process at work, let us suppose that you have to write a report on how far your organisation should take note of what research tells us makes written materials more legible and more readable. You will find in Appendix 11.1 some notes on this subject.

After studying this information, you might decide to ignore all the points about which a writer could not very easily do anything useful. On this basis, you might decide to ignore, under 'Legibility', points 1, 10 and 11. You might also decide to ignore points which did not refer to the writing, typing or printing of reports. In this case, you might also decide to ignore under the same heading points 6 and 9. Already you have begun to whittle the information that is available down to an amount that will meet your objective. You might also decide that some information is so basic that it must be included. You might then decide that the points which will feature particularly strongly in your report are numbers 5, 12, 15, 17, 18, 19 and 20.

Once you have selected the information you will use in your report, you can turn your attention to the structure of the report and to deciding which information will go into which section.

5.4 Arrangement of Information

You now have your report ready. Unfortunately, it is not yet in presentable form. All the information is to hand, but it has to be arranged in some kind of order before it can be written up. In Appendix 11.2, there is a list of all the possible parts which may go to make up a report. Few reports will need to use all these parts. Only very long, formal reports will use most of them. Many short, informal reports will comprise the following four elements:

1. Summary
2. Introduction
3. The Body of the Report (using appropriate headings)
4. Conclusions and/or Recommendations

You will need to choose the arrangement that is best suited to your report. Many variations are possible. It does not particularly matter what the arrangement is, so long as it is there. It needs to be logical and clear to the reader. At least one organisation uses an inverted form of this basic structure because it suits its purposes. Its reports take the form:

1. Conclusions and/or Recommendations – for readers who want only the bare essentials.
2. The Body of the Report – for readers who need to see how the conclusions and recommendations were arrived at.
3. Background – this is really an introductory section, placed towards the end of the report because it will only be read by those who need to have some background information about the subject before they can understand the body of the report. It can also be used to cover the history of a topic for those who need to be brought up to date.

4. Summary – provided at the end of the report for those readers in a hurry who still need an overall picture. It is unusual nowadays, however, for the summary to be placed at the end of the report. Normally, it is placed at the front for the convenience of the reader.

It is easier to achieve a logical arrangement for the information in the report if headings are used. Each section of the report (and this also applies to the parts of the body of the report) should be given a

PRIMARY HEADING

and each sub-section should be given a

Secondary Heading

and any further divisions of sub-sections which are necessary can be given a

Sub-heading

(You should note that the sub-heading is indented about five spaces).

Headings and sub-headings should be numbered or lettered and this should be done in such a way that each is clearly distinguishable. The most common method is the one used in this guide. it is called the 'decimal' system and works like this:

1.   PRIMARY HEADING

1.1 Secondary Heading

    1.1.1 Sub-heading
    1.1.2 Sub-heading

Some other possible arrangements are:

1.   PRIMARY HEADING

(a) Secondary Heading
   (i)   Sub-heading
   (ii) Sub-heading

1.   PRIMARY HEADING

2.   Secondary Heading
   3.   Sub-heading
   4.   Sub-heading

A.   PRIMARY HEADING

1.   Secondary Heading
   (a)   Sub-heading
   (b)   Sub-heading

PRIMARY HEADING

1.1 All paragraphs in a chapter are numbered in
    sequence. Any secondary headings which are
    necessary are inserted between paragraphs and are
    not numbered.
1.2 This pattern is used in many Government reports.

The use of a simple, clear system of identification
will make the report not only more readable, but also
much simpler to write. Placing and arranging material
under each heading will be made easier. Everything
will tend to fall much more naturally into its logical
position in the report.

5.5 Organising the Body of the Report

The body of each report will, of course, be unique,
according to its contents. Each will require individual
planning. Exceptions are pro forma reports and
certain other routine reports where a set structure

can be used every time.

Basically, you have to identify and label the several sections into which the body of the report can logically be divided. Again, it might help if we take an example: Suppose you are writing a report on the work of your department. The body of such a report might be divided into the following sections:

(i) Department activities in the past year
(ii) Significant achievements
(iii) Failures to meet targets
(iv) Suggested objectives for the year ahead

In this way, as for the report as a whole (see 5.4), your tasks of selection and arrangement are made easier. Preparing for ease and fluency of expression is, in fact, one of the main benefits of careful planning. This is especially true for those people, and there are many, who do not enjoy writing reports. Almost any chore can be made a little less unpleasant if it is planned properly in advance.

When planning the body of the report, you should never use as headings the terms 'Body of the Report' or 'Main Text'. These terms do not help the reader as much as a clear, specific heading of the kind illustrated both in the example above and, indeed, in this guide itself. Look at the table of contents in this guide and see how the body of it (sections 3 to 9 inclusive) has been broken into sections. Each section has a simple title which indicates clearly the nature of its contents.

5.6 Exercises

So that you can assess how well you are able to put the instruction given in this section into practice, it will be useful to attempt at least one of the following exercises:

  (i) Make a list of the types of reports you regularly have to write. Classify them as short (up to about six pages) or long (over six pages), and as informal (written for internal reading only and usually for an immediate superior, where clear, direct communication is more important than an impressive style and layout) or formal (usually written for an external readership or for higher management, where a simple, basic approach might be seen as 'writing down' to the readers).

 (ii) Using the information on legibility and readability given in Appendix 11.1, plan a report on how far your organisation should take note of what the available research has to say on this subject.

(iii) Plan, in detail, an inverted report on a visit to another location occupied by your organisation (if your organisation has no other locations assume a visit to another organisation).

(iv) For one of the reports planned in (ii) or (iii) above, try some of the methods of identifying (numbering or lettering) headings outlined in section 5.4. What are the relative advantages and disadvantages of each?

5.7 Completion Checklist

At the end of this section you should be able to deal with the following points:

  (i) What are the main types of reports that you have to write?

 (ii) What principles should be followed in selecting

the information that will go into the report?

(iii) What are the four elements of the basic structures of a report?

(iv) List all the possible parts which may go to make up a report.

(v) List the ways of identifying (numbering and lettering) headings given in this guide.

(vi) Why should you never use the term 'Body of the Report' (or 'Main Text') as a heading in a report?

6: Expression

Now that you have planned your report, you are ready
to begin writing it. For many report writers, this is
seen as the most difficult of the five stages. If you
have carried out the first three stages properly, you
will find that the problems of expression are much
reduced. Following the instruction and advice given
in this section will reduce them still further.

This section assumes that you already have some
experience of writing and some knowledge of how
language is structured. It assumes that you
understand terms like 'paragraph', 'sentence',
'clause', 'phrase', 'noun', 'verb', 'adjective', 'adverb',
and other basic grammatical terms. If your recollection
of the English grammar you were taught at school is
a little hazy, you may find it useful to refresh it by
looking at one of the grammar books listed under
'Further Reading' at the end of this guide. You should
do this, if you can, before you proceed with this
section.

If you wish at this point to make a general
assessment of your writing abilities, you will find it
useful to complete the Self-analysis of Writing Ability on
pages 40-41. Assess yourself as honestly as you can on
each point on the scale rating from −3 to +3. From
each pair take the statement which most applies to

you and mark an 'X' under the appropriate score. When you have finished connect all the 'Xs' together to form a profile. Add up all the plus scores; add up all the minus scores. Subtract the minus total from the plus total. If your overall score is lower than −5, you may well need to do some revision work on your use of language in order to benefit fully from this guide.

Example rating:

| −3 | −2 | −1 | 0 | +1 | +2 | +3 |

Has difficulty with spelling   Spells correctly

(i.e. This shows that a writer rates himself at −2 on point 12 in the list)

6.1 Task Checklist

During the writing stage you will need to:

(i) write the report within as short a period of time as possible;

(ii) write the parts of the report in the order recommended in this section;

(iii) follow the principles and techniques of effective writing as outlined in this section;

(iv) keep the report as short as possible, bearing in mind the amount of information it must contain;

(v) use appropriate illustrative material in the report;

(vi) keep the needs of your readers in mind at all times.

6.2 Rapid Composition

It is desirable to write a report within as short a period of time as possible. The longer the time taken to write a report, the more likely it is that you will alter your concept of what the report should be like. If, during the course of writing, you change your idea of how the report should be organised, the finished product is unlikely to be a complete and logical whole. You are more likely to confuse your readers by changes in intention or emphasis.

If you can tell from your planning that the report will be too long to be written at a single sitting, you should break the writing up into convenient parts. You should aim at least to complete a section or a number of sections at a sitting. Try to avoid leaving the writing in the middle of a section.

When you have to take a break, make sure that you have clear notes about what you will write when you return to your task. This will avoid sitting down and waiting for inspiration or searching for the right words with which to begin. It may even be helpful to write down the first sentence of the section you will return to. This will remind you of how you intend to proceed and will provide you with a useful starter. It will minimise the time needed to 'get back into the swing of things'.

As you write, do not worry too much about style or the quality of your writing. Concentrate on getting the information on to paper as quickly as possible. Let the words look after themselves. You will have the chance to make as many changes as you wish when you come to the Review stage of the report writing process. That is when you can amend, delete and add things in order to polish your writing so that it communicates efficiently and effectively.

Set yourself a deadline for the completion of the first draft of the report which will allow you enough time for revision and editing. This will probably mean that, if the report cannot be completed at a single sitting, you will need to group the sittings as closely together as possible. This will help you to maintain momentum and finish the writing without too many pauses in which you wonder what to write next. The main aim is that, once you have started, you should keep going until you finish. Concentrating the work in this way will actually make the whole task easier and more likely to succeed.

6.3 Order of Writing

The body of the report should be written first. This is the heart of the document and you will need it to hand before you can even begin to tackle some of the other sections.

The introduction should be written next. The function of the introduction, as we have seen, is to set out the purpose and scope of the report and to say how the subject will be treated. It is much easier to introduce something when you have it before you. If you try to write the introduction before writing the body, you may find that the body of the report does not take quite the form you originally thought. This will mean that you have introduced your reader to something that does not exist in the form you have described. You will then have to re-write your introduction.

SELF-ANALYSIS OF WRITING ABILITY

Poor Writer				Good Writer		
−3	−2	−1	0	+1	+2	+3

1. Does not always check the accuracy of what he has written.

   Makes sure that what he writes is accurate (i.e., that the facts are correct).

2. Does not control the length of what he writes

   Writes as briefly and concisely as the subject matter will allow.

3. His meaning is not always clear.

   Makes sure that his readers will clearly understand what he has written.

4. Pays little attention to keeping what he writes as simple as possible.

   Keeps what he writes as simple as the complexity of the content will allow.

5. Has no clear sense of purpose in writing

   Defines his purposes clearly before writing.

6. Is unable to suit the order and arrangement of what he has to say to his purposes in writing and the nature of the material to ensure effectiveness.

   Writes effectively by suiting the order and arrangement of what he has to say to his purposes in writing and the nature of the material itself.

7. Carries out preparatory work haphazardly and does not work to a plan.

   Prepares and plans his writing systematically.

8. Is unable to change his style of writing to suit different purposes or materials.

   Has the flexibility to change his style of writing to suit different purposes and materials.

9. His writing contains many common structural and grammatical errors.

   Writes correctly, within the limits allowed by currently acceptable usage.

10. Writes only when he cannot avoid it.

    Enjoys writing and has experience of a wide range of writing activities.

11. Has a limited vocabulary.

    Has a wide and constantly developing vocabulary.

SELF-ANALYSIS OF WRITING ABILITY

Poor Writer				Good Writer		
−3	−2	−1	0	+1	+2	+3

12. Has difficulty in spelling correctly.

Spells correctly.

13. Has difficulty in punctuating his writing effectively.

Uses appropriate punctuation with ease and effectiveness.

14. His writing has no identifiable style and is not easy to read rapidly and efficiently.

Has a range of clearly identifiable personal writing styles which can be read rapidly and efficiently.

15. Writes illegibly.

Writes legibly.

16. Has limited general background of knowledge and experience

Has a broad general background of knowledge and experience and a thoughtful and critical approach to both.

Then the conclusions and/or recommendations should be written. These are, by definition, opinions. Therefore, they should be kept clear of the facts of the report as given in the body. Sometimes, however, they may have to be stated in the sections from which they derive. You will have to be particularly careful, if this is the case, to differentiate facts from opinions. Otherwise, you will risk misleading your readers, or at the very least confusing them. You will still need to re-state them in a separate conclusions and/or recommendations section for the convenience of readers, so this will help you to avoid mixing the two indiscriminately.

Appendices, references and other remaining parts of the report can be dealt with next. Much of this information will have been acquired and written down or produced in graphic form during the preparation stage. All that is required here is to make sure that appendices appear in the order in which they are referred to in the body of the report. References should be listed in alphabetical order.

The last part of the report to be written is the summary, even though it will usually appear first in the finished report. The reason for leaving it until last is that it is impossible to summarise anything properly until you have the whole of it before you. The summary should contain the highlights or essential points of the report, regardless of which section or appendix they appear in.

6.4 Implementing the Plan

It is inadvisable to begin tampering with the plan during the writing of the report. If you have come this far and then discover that the plan you started with is faulty, you have only two choices: either you must scrap the plan and start stage three from scratch or you can continue with the faulty plan. If you choose the latter, you will be able to make any changes in the structure of the report during he review stage. It may even be easier to carry out this kind of 'scissors and paste' job than to try to start afresh. If you are working with a word processor, this task will be much easier.

Whether you decide to go back or to continue may well depend on how long the report is and how far you have progressed with it before you discover your mistake. There will be a 'point of no return' which you will have to judge for yourself. If it does happen, you will find it useful to spend a little time trying to identify the source of your error. This will help you to avoid the same mistake in future. There is benefit even in failure if it is exploited properly. Lessons learned in the hard school of experience are also unlikely to be forgotten.

6.5 Effective Writing

As was said at the beginning of this section, you are assumed to have a basic competence in using language. What are offered here are some principles and techniques for improving upon that basic competence in the quest for more effectively written reports.

Keep your readers firmly in mind as you write and you will be much less likely to disappoint them. You will produce material upon which they can base sound decisions and take appropriate action.

You will also write more effectively if you have a writing strategy which lists good writing practices in order of importance. A systematic approach is as important in writing as it is in preparation, assessment and planning and it will be just as necessary when you come to review what you have written. Approach your writing in the following stages:

Firstly, you should have an overall approach to writing tasks. This you are currently developing, as you progress through the five stage approach to report writing in this guide. This approach can, of course, be used in the production of any kind of written material.

Secondly, you should make sure the pattern of organisation you choose suits your purpose in writing and the nature of the material to be communicated. We shall return to this point in section 6.5.6 below.

The next area to attend to is that of paragraph construction. Ideas and information should be grouped together into sequences that will form the basis of paragraphs. You should take care to ensure that each paragraph will deal with a unified set of facts or ideas.

Then you should consider how you will construct the sentences which will make up the paragraph. You will need to identify the key or topic sentence of each paragraph and will need to preserve the unity and agreement of each sentence. That is to say, each sentence can only have one subject and the verb and its tense must agree and remain consistent.

Fifthly, you should pay attention to style. This is not to advocate a 'literary' approach to report writing, but merely to remind you that we all have individual writing styles, just as we all have individual speaking styles. Style is determined by every item in this hierarchy, but choice of words is the single most important influence upon it. A style which habitually chooses long words in preference to short ones will be very different from one which does the opposite. Nor does everyone have a single style. We have many, ranging from the very casual style of personal letters to the highly formal style of a letter, say, to the Inland Revenue.

The next area for attention is the grammatical appropriateness of whatever you write. Even where there are no strict rules there are usually conventions about how language can be used and how it cannot.

Seventhly, punctuation must be used in such a way that it assists rather than hinders the communication of information and ideas. It should be kept as simple as possible. Tempting though it is to sprinkle colons and semi-colons around like confetti, you can do a great deal by using only full stops and commas.

Lastly, you need to attend to spelling. It may not appear to matter too much if the odd word is misspelled, but readers may well doubt the soundness of the information you give them if you cannot master a small technicality like spelling.

Although this list of the eight areas for attention in using a systematic approach to writing is a hierarchy, in that it is more important to attend to the ones at the top of the list than the ones at the bottom, it is not intended to imply that the items at the bottom of the list are unimportant. All of these items are important. It is simply that some are more important than others.

6.5.1 *Style*

Let us return to the fifth point in the hierarchy: style. There are numerous ways in which you can bring an individuality to whatever you write which will not only enable you to communicate more effectively with other people, but also give your writing extra colour and impact at the same time.

A careful choice of words can enable you to convey many subtleties of meaning. One tool which can help you to achieve this is a thesaurus. A dictionary tells you the meaning of a word, a thesaurus tells you several words which will convey a particular meaning. Or it may be that you are searching for just the right word which will express exactly what you want to say; a thesaurus will help you to do this as well. This makes a thesaurus as essential a tool for every report writer as a dictionary.

There are many informal reports where it will be sufficient for you to call a spade a spade, but you need to be prepared for those other occasions on which it is better to call it a shovel. You should, therefore, be prepared to avoid the commonplace if it will add to the quality of your writing. You should always strive to adjust your style to your readers and avoid 'writing down' (or 'writing up') to them. You need to develop a sensitivity to those occasions which require a more formal approach and to those where informality is better.

In developing your awareness of the complexities of the relationships between form and content, you will try to select words which will blend both of them together into an effective whole. You will find this easier to achieve if you get into the habit of reading widely. Your reading does not have to be related to your job to help in this: indeed, it is better if it is not. People who only read what they have to in the course of their work will find it very difficult to develop into effective writers. No one can say exactly why it is that wide reading helps to enhance writing skills, but there is no doubt that it does.

6.5.2 Accuracy

You should check that everything you write is factually accurate. The facts should be capable of being verified. Moreover, arguments should be soundly based and your reasoning should be logical. You should write nothing that will misinform, mislead or unfairly persuade your readers. If you do, you will be doing a disservice not only to yourself but also to the organisation and, possibly, its customers. Accurate information is essential for effective communication and decision making.

It is tempting sometimes to take short-cuts. If you are writing as a specialist for non-specialists, which is often the case where a technical expert is writing for general management, you may feel that you can make statements which you would not make for a technical readership, in order, perhaps, to press a case. The danger with such approaches is that you only have to be found out once for your entire credibility to be destroyed or at the very least to be undermined.

There is an old saying that liars must have good memories. Certainly, it is much easier to write honestly and fairly. This makes for an enhanced personal reputation as well as for more efficient organisational running. Accurate reports, then, are not only more useful to their readers, they also reduce the writer's problems in expressing himself.

6.5.3 Conciseness

Julius Caesar, when he conquered Britain, reported: 'Veni, vidi, vici.' (I came, I saw, I conquered.) None of your reports will be as brief as his three words. You should still aim, though, at keeping your reports as short as possible. In doing this, you should not mistake brevity for conciseness. A report may be brief because it omits important information. A concise report, on the other hand, is short but still contains all the essential details.

To make sure that you do not go beyond this and include material which can safely be left out, you should not ask: Can this information be left out? Rather, you should ask: Must this information be included? In this way, you will be sure to put into your report only so much information as your readers need in order to respond as you wish them to.

Keeping the average length of sentences short helps to achieve conciseness. Aim for an *average* sentence length of *less than* 20 words. This does not mean, of course, that every sentence in a section must contain no more than 20 words. In fact, it is preferable to vary the lengths and constructions of sentences, otherwise your writing will have a staccato rhythm or a terseness which many readers may find either childish or otherwise irritating. (That sentence has 34 words.)

(This sub-section has an average sentence length of 16 words.)

6.5.4 Clarity and Consistency

One of the best ways to achieve clarity in your writing is to allow a period of at least twenty-four hours to elapse between the first draft and its revision. If you can leave it for longer, so much the better. If you are really under pressure and it simply is not possible to leave it overnight, at least try to leave it over a lunch or coffee break. It is vital that you should have a period of time, no matter how small, when you can think of other things. In this way, when you come back to the report, you can look at it with a degree of objectivity. This break is, in fact, an incubation period (see section 4.2).

You can, however, increase your chances of writing with clarity and consistency if, as you write, you try to keep certain things in mind. Concentrate on your mental picture of your readers and make sure you are writing for them and not just for yourself. Make sure you write within the limits of what is grammatically correct. On points where grammatical authorities disagree, aim for what is conventionally acceptable. An example of this is in the use of the split infinitive. It used to be regarded as a fault if you were to unthinkingly split (that is an instance) an infinitive. Nowadays, if it makes the meaning flow better, it is permissible. Wherever possible, though, and especially if you know you are writing for someone who is a bit of a stickler for tradition, it is better always to avoid (that is an instance of not splitting) doing it.

If you are able to have your first draft read by a sympathetic colleague, this is a better way of ensuring clarity and consistency. It means that you are getting a genuine second opinion on your work.

6.5.5 *Simplicity*

Usually, if your writing is accurate, concise, clear, and consistent, it will also be as simple as it can be. You should guard against over-simplifying, that is, simplifying to the point of missing out information that your reader needs to understand fully what you are trying to tell him. Assuming you have avoided this, you should again keep your readership firmly in mind and keep asking yourself whether or not they will be able to follow the logic of your presentation.

Many difficulties in communicating are caused by making things more difficult than they need be. Many writers also over-estimate the reading abilities of those they are writing for. They forget that the average manager has a reading speed of about 225 words per minute and comprehends only about 75 per cent of what he reads. This is why this guide places so much emphasis on the need for a summary at the beginning of a report. Even if a reader is going to read the whole report, the summary tells him the essential points being made. It is always easier for a reader to process information when he has some knowledge of it in advance.

The problem of how to keep things simple is particularly acute for the technical writer. The information he has to convey is difficult for the non-technical reader to understand. If he simplifies his expression too much he may distort the meaning of whatever he is trying to say. It is all too easy for him to shrug his shoulders at this and tell himself that it is not his fault and his readers will just have to follow him as best they can. This is simply not good enough. Even the technical writer has to make every effort to serve his readers.

They are, after all, the really important people. If they do not understand, they will reject what he has to say. If he depends on their approval to a course of action he is helping neither them nor himself by refusing to take their limitations into account. No writer can afford to be so self-indulgent.

There are plenty of examples to be found of writers who have discovered a way to make difficult content easier to assimilate. Read the science writer Nigel Calder, for instance, and see how he can make even abstract concepts intelligible to the layman. It can be done. It just takes a little effort.

The rewards of writing simply are considerable. Readers are more likely to respond favourably to conclusions drawn and proposals made. At the very least they are more likely to understand what is being said to them. They will form a higher opinion of the writer himself. They will read subsequent reports, written by a writer who has clearly gone out of his way to help them, with greater attention and enthusiasm. They may even, in time, be educated into understanding more difficult technical information. When a writer achieves this, he has become more than a writer. He has become a teacher. He has increased his capacity to guide and influence those with, and for whom, he works. It is an achievement not to be undervalued.

6.5.6 Patterns of Organisation

Some of the objectives for clarity, consistency and simplicity can be achieved through choosing the best way of organising your material. To do this, you should pay particular attention to identifying the type of writing you will be using, to structuring your paragraphs and sentences for maximum effect, and to ordering the points to be made in the manner most likely to make them succeed in communicating with your readers. Let us look at each of these points more closely.

There are four types of writing: description, exposition, argument and narrative. In most materials, these types will be mixed, but one will be dominant and set the general tone and style. You should be familiar with each of these types of writing, try to identify them in the writing of others and be aware which type you are using every time you write.

In description, you try to create a picture which your readers can see in their minds. Key words, phrases and statements will be those which refer to colour, shape, size, and appearance generally. It is important for you to be extra careful in choosing the right words to convey as accurate a picture as possible.

This will help readers to recreate in their minds whatever it is you are trying to describe. A thesaurus will be particularly useful here.

In exposition, you explain how something works, or give the facts about a situation, or make some other kind of statement. You need to organise your material so that it proceeds logically, step by step from stage to stage. Much instructional material is expository in nature, like this guide to report writing. You will also have to take care not to omit anything that the reader might need to understand the relationship of one part of the material to another.

Argument is the type of writing in which a case for or against something is being put forward, or where ideas are being discussed, or conclusions are being drawn, or recommendations are being made. It is essentially opinion, though it will be supported by factual evidence. You will help your readers if you keep the points supporting a case separate from those against it. You should also be careful not to mix facts and opinions indiscriminately.

In narrative, you are essentially setting out to tell a story. You give the details of a sequence of events, usually in chronological order or in movement from place to place. You have to be careful not to miss any significant events. You also have to avoid going too far towards the other extreme by including too many small and unimportant details. The aim should be to move fairly quickly through the story, as it were, from the beginning to the end.

Whatever the type of writing, you will need to arrange the main points to be made into paragraphs. It is worth remembering that long paragraphs, like long sentences, take longer to read and that if readers take longer to read something they are more likely to misunderstand it.

It should be possible to break your information into parts of such a size that long paragraphs are avoided. Shorter paragraphs make for easier, faster and better reading. As a rough guide, any paragraph with more than about a dozen lines in should be examined to see if it can be broken into two or more smaller paragraphs. You should avoid, however, splitting a paragraph for the sake of it. As with sentences, variety in construction and length is more important than brevity alone. As long as the average length of paragraphs is about 5-10 lines (again a rule-of-thumb measurement only), this should make them about right for reasonably efficient reading.

Usually, each paragraph will contain one sentence which expresses the main point the paragraph will develop. This key, or topic, sentence should be placed at either the beginning or the end of the paragraph. The reason for this is that the beginning of a paragraph and, to a lesser extent, the end, carry a natural emphasis. It is logical, therefore, to put sentences which are important in a place of natural emphasis. If key sentences are tucked away in the middle of paragraphs, their importance may not be realised. They may even be missed altogether by a reader.

It is a useful exercise to take a paragraph you have written and write each sentence out on a small piece of paper. You can then move these pieces of paper about to see what the effect is of placing sentences in different positions. A similar exercise can be carried out with a sentence. You should aim to see in how many different ways the sentence can be written without changing the meaning.

In deciding how to order the points you wish to make in the most effective way, it is worth your while to consider the various choices open to you. There are at least six different ways that occur frequently in reports. These are:

(i) Chronological order. Best suited to narrative.

(ii) The order of ascending importance, in which the main points comes last. This is effective when you want your main argument to be the last one your readers see.

(iii) The order of descending importance, in which the main point comes first. You would use this when you wish your main argument to make an initial impact on your readers.

(iv) Moving from the general to the particular. If you were describing a location you had visited, this would be one way to do it.

(v) Moving from the particular to the general. If you were seeking to make a general point arising out of some specific examples, this is the order you would use.

(vi) By area or aspect of a subject. This is a common pattern in exposition where things have to be broken into assimilable amounts and yet a logical ordering has to be maintained.

It is quite possible, of course, that in a report you may use different methods of ordering the material in different sections. This does not matter. What is important is that the method of ordering information should suit your purpose in writing and the nature of the information you are dealing with.

6.5.7 *Some Practical Tips for Effective Writing*

There are several well-known and well-tried pieces of
advice to writers. Most of them apply to report writing
as much as to the writing of anything else. You will
find it useful to keep them in mind whenever you are
writing. Remember, though, that they are simply
pieces of sound advice based upon the experience of
many other writers and readers. They represent rules
which can be broken if there is a good reason for
breaking them. This is the key. You only really need
to worry if the responses of your readers indicate that
you are breaking rules without realising that you are
breaking them. These are not golden rules. The golden-
rule about language is that there are no golden rules.
You can even begin a sentence with a conjunction. If
you wish. If you will achieve an effect you could not
otherwise achieve. If you know you are doing it.

In the pieces of advice which follow, the faulty or
defective sentence appears first as (i) and the corrected
or improved sentence appears second as (ii)

(a) Omit unnecessary words from sentences.
   (i) The resolution and determination of the
      management were admired and praised by the
      workers.
   (ii) The determination of the management was
      praised by the workers.

(b) Use direct statement with active verbs in
   preference to the passive voice.
   (i) The determination of the management was
      praised by the workers.
   (ii) The workers praised the determination of the
      management.

(c) Omit qualifying phrases unless they are essential
   to the sense of sentences.
   (i) The workers, somewhat enthusiastically in the

circumstances, praised the determination of
the management.

  (ii) The workers praised the determination of the
    management.

(d) Keep sentences short (but remember what has
 already been said about variety in construction
 being more important than brevity).

  (i) The workers, who had never had to work so
    hard before, praised the determination of the
    management.

  (ii) The workers praised the determination of the
    management. The workers had never had to
    work so hard before.

(e) Change long words and phrases to shorter ones
 where possible.

  (i) The artisans expressed their admiration of the
    indefatigability of the functionaries under
    whose supervision they laboured.

  (ii) The workers praised the determination of the
    management.

(f) Make sure you know the exact meanings of the
 words you use and use them in appropriate
 contexts.

  (i) The workers exalted the determination of the
    management.

  (ii) The workers praised the determination of the
    management.

(g) Preserve the unity of each sentence and each
 paragraph. In other words, each sentence should
 have one subject and each paragraph should deal
 with a single topic.

  (i) The workers praised the determination and
    the directors admired the business planning of
    the management.

  (ii) The workers praised the determination of the
    management. The directors admired the

management's business planning.

(h) No apology for reminding you once again to keep your readers in mind all the time you are writing. Write for them. Keep asking yourself: Will they understand this?

Here is a selection of practical tips for writers, each of which is in itself a demonstration of the fault it is describing:

Avoid run-on sentences they are hard to read.

Do not use no double negatives.

Verbs has to agree with their subjects.

No sentence fragments.

Proofread carefully to see if you any words out.

Avoid commas, that are not necessary.

If you reread your work, you will find on rereading that a great deal of repetition can be avoided by rereading and editing.

A writer must not shift your point of view.

Do not overuse exclamation marks!!!

Place pronouns as close as possible, especially in long sentences as of ten or more words, to their antecedents.

Hyphenate between syllables and avoid un-necessary hyphens.

Don't use contractions in formal writing.

Writing carefully, unrelated participles must be avoided.

It is incumbent upon us to avoid archaic words.

Everyone should be careful to use a singular pronoun with singular nouns in their writing.

Also, avoid awkward or affected alliteration.

"Avoid overuse of 'quotation "marks"'."

Last but not least, avoid clichés like the plague; seek viable alternatives.

6.6 Length

Those who are new to report writing often ask: How long should a report be? There is no simple answer to the question other than to reply: Only as long as necessary.

There are no set or expected lengths for different kinds of reports. A formal report does not have to be a long one. An informal report may be longer than many formal ones.

So long as the report deals properly with all the matters it is supposed to deal with, it can be any length from less than a page to hundreds of pages. Typically, however, the usual lengths for some common kinds of reports will be as follows:

Kind of Report	Number of Pages	Number of Words
Visit	1 – 4	300 – 1,200
Accident	1 – 2	300 – 600
Inspection	1 – 2	Usually mainly ticks in boxes
Laboratory	2 – 6	500 – 2,000
Sales	1 – 5	300 – 1,500
Test	1 – 2	Similar to inspection reports
Technical investigation	2 – 10	500 – 3,000
Management	1 – 10	300 – 3,000
Reports on people	1 – 4	300 – 1,200
Projects	6 – 200	1,500 – 80,000
Reports on meetings	1 – 4	300 – 1,200
Feasibility study	10 – hundreds	3,000 – 100,000+
Survey	10 – 50	3,000 – 15,000
Research	5 – 20	1,500 – 6,000

Remember that these are not recommended lengths. They are only typical lengths. It may be, however, that if most of your reports fall at the lower end of a range they may be too short and you may be omitting information your readers need. If your reports are nearly all at the upper end, you may either be giving them too much information or your reports may be unnecessarily verbose. You will have to make your own judgement on this point.

6.7 Illustrative Material

Unless they are either brief, compact or an integral part of a section, graphs, tables and other illustrative materials should be relegated to an appendix. If you give a clear cross-reference, your readers should have no difficulty in finding them.

When preparing illustrations, you should consider carefully which method of graphic communication best suits your purpose. The examples given below will show you some of the possibilities.

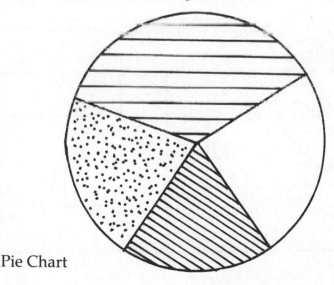

Pie Chart

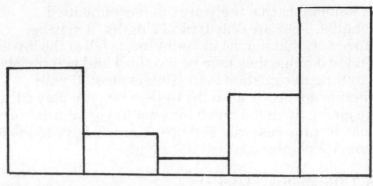

Bar Chart (or Histogram)

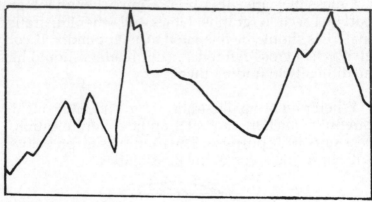

Graph

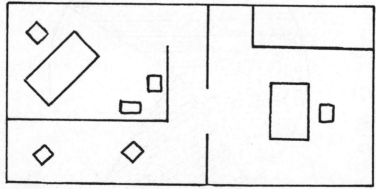

Plan

6.8 Exercises

So that you can assess how well you are able to put the instruction given in this section into practice, it will be useful to attempt at least one of the following exercises:

 (i) Suppose you had to write a report on a subject for which you required little or no preparation (say, on your current workload) during the course of the next week, how much time would you have to do it? Make out a diary of your activities at work for the week ahead, breaking each day into 30-minute periods.

 (ii) Obtain a dictionary and a thesaurus. Select a word in the dictionary at random. Then turn to the thesaurus and see how many words you can find, first of similar meaning, then of opposite meaning.

(iii) Calculate your own reading speed and comprehension level, using a textbook in rapid reading. This author's 'Rapid Reading Made Simple' (published by Heinemann) will show you how to do this. From this you may gain some insight into average reading abilities.

(iv) Re-write the following paragraph so as to simplify it without changing the meaning:

The product configuration baseline necessitates that urgent consideration be applied to the evolution of specifications over a given time period. In respect to specific goals, the characterisation of specific criteria presents extremely interesting challenges to the greater profitability concept. As a resultant implication, the fully integrated test programme effects a significant implementation to the system rationale.

(v) Identify the dominant type of writing in each of the following paragraphs:

(a) The factory is situated near the southern boundary of the industrial estate. Access is difficult as the county council has not yet completed the road network in this area. Lorries have to enter at the northern end of the estate and make their way through narrow and often obstructed roads. The factory itself, however, is of modern design and offers a pleasant working environment for both management and workforce.

(b) Despite the drawbacks at present, it will probably be advantageous to remain at this location. When the roads are complete and all other environmental works have been finished, this will be one of the most attractive factories in the company's ownership. I would recommend that, for the time being at least, we take no action on the proposal to consider relocation.

(c) I approached the site from the perimeter road. As I drew level with the main gate, I saw the articulated container truck attempt to enter the rather narrow gate. The trailer, however, caught the left hand gate post and demolished it. The driver appeared to be unaware of the damage he had caused, as he continued into the site and drove round to the loading bays at the rear.

(d) The process undertaken at the plant is highly automated. Raw material is delivered at one end of the long building. Once this is loaded into the hoppers, it progresses through the various stages completely automatically. The finished products emerge at the other end of the building, ready for loading and dispatch.

(vi) Using the paragraphs in (v) above, re-arrange the sentences in each to see what effect this has on the meaning.

(vii) Re-write the following sentence in as many different ways as you can without significantly changing the meaning:

The prime responsibility for maintaining effective communication within an organisation belongs to management.

(viii) Apply the practical tips outlined in section 6.5.7 to the following paragraph:

A report is an ordered and logical statement, with appropriate use of sectional headings and sub-headings, of the facts about a situation or problem, the case for and against a proposed course of action, the likely or actual effects of a decision or course of action, a description and evaluation of the results of work or research, or a record of a sequence of events, with interpretation of the significance of specific events within the sequence, together with any necessary resultant conclusions and/or recommendations, and any supporting evidence, illustrative materials, or other appendices. Normally, the report will be prefaced by a brief summary.

6.9 Completion Checklist

At the end of this section you should be able to answer the following questions:

(i) Why is it desirable to write a report within as short a period of time as possible?

63

(ii) In which order should the various parts of a report be written?

(iii) What choices do you have if you begin writing and find that your plan is defective?

(iv) What are the eight elements of the writing strategy outlined in this section?

(v) What basic reference book do all report writers need in addition to a dictionary?

(vi) What are the four types of writing?

(vii) Name six different ways of ordering information.

(viii) List eight practical tips for effective writing.

(ix) What should you keep in mind at all times?

7: Review

We now come to the fifth and final stage in the process of producing a report. The report is written, but it is only in first draft. It has to be checked for errors and omissions and many other things. It has to be edited and brought into its final shape. It has to be assessed for readability and the expression polished until you are satisfied that it is the best report you can write on the subject.

In many ways, the report is far from finished. The review stage is a vital element in your report writing strategy. It is a mistake to think that, once a report is written, that is the end of it. In some senses, it is only the beginning.

7.1 Task Checklist

During the review stage you will need to:

 (i) carry out a detailed report analysis;
 (ii) assess the readability of the report;
 (iii) edit the report and polish the expression;
 (iv) decide the layout and method of reproducing or printing the report;
 (v) submit the complete report.

7.2 Report Analysis

In conducting the analysis, it will be helpful if you ask yourself the kind of questions suggested in this section. You should be prepared to re-write a report, or parts of it, rather than submit it in a form with which you are not completely satisfied.

It is best to carry out the analysis in two stages. First of all, you should check the meaning conveyed by the report. This may be called a semantic check. You are making sure that what the report actually says is what you intended it to say. Secondly, you should check the organisation and the technical details of expression (grammar, syntax, punctuation, spelling, etc.) in the report. This may be called a structural check. The two checks have to be made separately because it is extremely difficult, if not impossible, to check the flow of meaning at the same time as you are checking correctness or appropriateness of expression.

(a) Semantic Check
   (i) Are there any unnecessary repetitions?
  (ii) Is each section complete in itself?
 (iii) Is any section irrelevant?
 (iv) Have any details been overlooked?
  (v) Is there any ambiguity?
 (vi) Have you kept your readers in mind and written for them?
 (vii) Does the report read smoothly and is it a complete and logical whole?
(viii) Does the title accurately describe the contents of the report?
 (ix) Have the objectives been achieved and the

terms of reference fulfilled?

(x) Are there any contradictions?

(xi) Are facts clearly differentiated from opinions?

(xii) Do any parts of the report pose legal problems (for example, possible libel or breaches of security)? This aspect should be checked with the legal department if such problems are likely to arise.

(xiii) Are all conclusions and recommendations clearly justified by the facts given?

(xiv) Will readers understand the report and has a check for readability been made (see 7.3)?

(xv) Going through the report in detail, can any words, phrases, statements, paragraphs or sections be omitted without loss or do any need to be changed to simplify and clarify the meaning?

(xvi) Have the principles and techniques of effective writing been followed to the best of your ability?

(xvii) Can the summary be read and understood without reference to the rest of the report?

(xviii) Have you avoided jargon as far as possible? Is a glossary of terms needed?

(xix) If you received this report, would you be able to deal with it? Would you know just what decisions were required? Would you appreciate the practical consequences? Would you know who else might be affected?

(xx) Have you considered any necessary security precautions if the report is confidential?

(xxi) Is any of the information more suitable for presentation as a diagram or graph or other visual form?

(xxii) Have you taken account of any minority or dissenting opinions? Should these be included in an appendix?

(b) Structural Check

   (i) Is each section in its proper place?

  (ii) Is any section badly planned?

 (iii) Is the structure of the report right for the job it has to do?

 (iv) Are there any parts of the body of the report where some information should be taken out and put into an appendix?

  (v) Have the punctuation and spelling been checked?

 (vi) Is the layout attractive?

(vii) If the report is long or detailed, will an index help the reader?

(viii) Have you written with grammatical correctness or appropriateness?

 (ix) Are you satisfied with your paragraph and sentence structure?

  (x) If the report is typewritten, are there any typographical errors?

 (xi) Are you completely satisfied with the completed report? If you have time, check it again or ask someone else to check it.

Not all of these questions will be relevant to every report. You should ask yourself as many of them as are relevant. You can, of course, add other questions to the list if required.

When you come to check the final draft of the report, many of these questions can be used again. You will find that, for this last check, it will be useful if you can enlist the services of someone else. One of you should read the report aloud and check that the meaning flows as it should. The other should follow the typed or printed text and check the technical details of expression, such as punctuation, spelling, grammar and so on. If no one else is available to help you to do this, read the report into a tape recorder and then follow the text yourself as you listen to the playback.

7.3 Assessing Readability

There are some notes on the elements of readability, legibility and how to make written materials more readable in Appendix 11.1. One method of encouraging readability is to see that the material passes a readability measurement. There are many ways of doing this and the one chosen will largely depend on personal preference.

(a) *Gunning's Fog Index*

This is so called because it tells you how 'foggy' or lacking in clarity your writing is. The answer you get in using the formula tells you roughly how many years of schooling someone will need to read your material with ease and understanding.

The steps of the calculation are:

(i) Count a sample of 100 words. Divide this by the number of sentences. This gives you the average sentence length (e.g. $100 \div 4 = 25$).

(ii) In the same sample, count the number of polysyllabic words (words which have three or more syllables). Do not count words which begin with capital letters, words that are combinations of short, easy words (e.g., book-keeper, troubleshooter), or words that are made into three syllables by adding '-ed' or '-es' (e.g., expected, services).

(iii) Add the two results together and multiply by 0.4 (e.g., $(25+5)\times0.4=12$).

Applied to a range of reading materials, the Fog Index has given the following results:

The Times	=	10.7
Daily Mirror	=	9.2
Beatrix Potter	=	7.9
Hemingway	=	10.7
A business report	=	12.2
HMSO report	=	15.2

(b) *'Cloze' Procedure*

A cloze is a gap in written material created by removing a word. How well a reader can replace the missing words when several clozes are present gives an indication of how easy or difficult something is to read.

The steps of the procedure are:

(i) Count a sample of 100 words.

(ii) Delete every tenth word.

(iii) Ask a number of people among a potential readership to take part in an experiment in the effectiveness of communication in your organisation. Have them complete the passage by replacing the missing words (all gaps should be made the same length).

(iv) Score the completed passages for accuracy in replacing the missing words. Allow synonyms, but not words which fit yet change the original meaning.

Results: 7–10 correctly replaced: Easy to read.
   4– 6 correctly replaced: Difficult to read.
   0– 3 correctly replaced: Unreadable.

Cloze technique is used both as a method of assessing readability and also as a method of building up 'word sensitivity' in children and others who need to develop their reading skills.

(c) *Information Density*

This technique tells a writer if he is trying to convey too much information too quickly.

The steps in the calculation:

(i) Count a sample of 100 words.

(ii) Count the number of nouns and adjectives.

(iii) Express these as % of the total words.

Results: Over 50%: Increasing density and
       difficulty.
   30%-50%: Average difficulty.
   Below 30%: Increasingly easy to read.

A word of caution: too little information will, however, make the material worthless from the point of view of communicating usefully with your readers.

Although a single 100-word sample will give an indication of readability, it is better to take at least three samples and then calculate the average of the three. Samples should be chosen from near (but not at) the beginning, from the middle and from near (but not at) the end. It is preferable to avoid beginnings and endings because these usually have a slightly different structure from the rest of a piece of writing. For instance, they often have a higher number of short sentences and may therefore be untypical. If you rely on these, you may think your material is more readable than it actually is.

After using the report analysis checklist in 7.2 and after assessing for readability, using one of the techniques outlined here, you should re-write any parts which fail to pass muster. You should then check the material again to be sure.

7.4 Editing

The business of editing is easier with a typewritten draft than with a handwritten one. For this reason, if you are not a competent two-finger typist yourself, it is worthwhile asking for a typed draft from your secretary or from the typing pool. However, now that keyboard skills are becoming increasingly important it is worth learning to type yourself. The importance of this point will become still clearer in section 7.6 on using word processors. It does not take long to develop an acceptable degree of skill in using a keyboard. Many people find that with a little practice they can type noticeably faster than they can write.

One advantage in typing first drafts yourself is that you can indicate more clearly how you would like the final draft to be set out. This improves the communication between writer and typist and makes the work of both much easier.

When editing the first draft, it is important for you to bear in mind all of the questions set out in 7.2. In particular, you should make sure that you are still satisfied with your use of English. You should make sure that you have spelled words consistently throughout. Indeed, your whole use of language should be consistent. Beware of changing the point of view without good reason. Similarly, avoid changes in tense from past to present and vice versa. Make sure that the contents of each section agree with the headings you have used. Be careful that the logic and argument are consistent and that you do not have one section contradicting another.

If you have done your work properly so far, all of these points should have been taken care of. They are emphasised here because of their importance in ensuring that you produce reports which are a pleasure to read as well as sound functional pieces of written communication.

If your organisation has a manual of style which it expects all report writers to follow, make sure that you are familiar with it. If it does not have such a manual, there are several common conventions which you might find it worthwhile to follow.

Avoid abbreviations where you can. If you do use them, make sure that you write the term out in full the first time it appears with the abbreviation in brackets after it, as in 'Regional Development Grant (RDG)'.

It is usual to spell in full numbers up to nine, unless they are part of a sequence of statistics, say, percent ges. Often, larger round figures are written out, for example, 'twenty', 'hundred', 'a million'.

If you quote from someone else's work, use single quotation marks and where a quotation appears within a quotation use double quotation marks, as in: One training officer said, 'We use what our managing director calls an "experiential" approach.'

Avoid capitals, except for proper nouns. Be sparing

in your use of brackets and do not underline unless you wish the words to be put into italics when a report is being printed.

Consider what kinds of information may be better conveyed graphically and avoid tables of figures for the sake of including them. Whatever methods you do use should be simple so as not to defeat the object of including them, that is, to make the reader's task easier. It is also worth trying to use several methods of presenting information as this tends to add life and interest to a report.

The main tasks in editing are to put into effect what has been learned from the report analysis and the assessment of readability, to 'polish' the expression and to do whatever else is necessary to make the report ready for final typing. In one sense, it is possible to go on polishing for ever, because there is no such thing as a perfect piece of communication. However, at some point, you will have to tell yourself that you have done as much as can be done in the time available. On most occasions, time limitations will force you to take less time over editing than you would like. If you unexpectedly find that you have more time, you should use it. You should never allow yourself to sit back and think that there are no more improvements you can make. If ever you feel that what you have written is perfect, it almost certainly is not.

If time does permit, you should insert another incubation period into the report writing process at this point. Put the report on one side for at least twenty-four hours, preferably longer, and then go through it again. You will usually find that there are still ways in which your report can be improved. Even if you have not been consciously thinking about the report during the incubation period, the same kinds of mental processes we spoke of earlier will have been taking place. At the very least you will be able to look at your work with a greater degree of objectivity than is possible without an incubation period.

7.5 Layout and Presentation

Some very informal reports may quite suitably be submitted to the reader in handwritten form. Most business and industrial reports, though, will be typewritten. If several copies are needed for circulation and filing, this will certainly be the case.

It will be advisable for you to submit the final draft soon enough before the submission deadline to allow for any re-typing to be done.

Short reports of up to about half a dozen pages will not require binding and pages can simply be stapled together. Even so, it can improve the appearance of the report to insert it in a simple clear plastic folder. Simple touches like this are more effective than elaborate methods of presentation. If the method of presentation is too colourful, it may make a reader doubt the quality of the informational content.

A similar principle applies to longer and more formal reports, but these are usually placed in some kind of binder. A stiff cover and back sheet with the report between and the whole kept in place with a sprung plastic strip down the left hand edge is a common and attractive method. Strong staples down the left hand side, covered by black adhesive tape, or spiral bindings is another possibility.

As far as general layout is concerned, again, you should follow the house-style manual if there is one. If there is not, there are some conventions which most organisations now seem to follow. Reports should be typed on A4 paper, preferably on one side of the paper only. This makes the report easier to handle when reading it and also enables a reader to make his own notes or comments on the reverse sides.

Margins should be generous for the same reasons. They are not necessary for readability, according to the research, but they do improve the appearance of documents. Allow at least 1½ inches at the top and down the left hand side and at least 1 inch at the bottom and down the right hand side.

All main sections should begin on a new page and each page should be numbered, usually in the top right hand corner. This helps a reader particularly in a long report where he may need to find a page in a hurry.

Ideally, beginnings of paragraphs should be indented. As Appendix 11.1 points out, this is what research tells us is desirable. In fact, where paragraphs are not indented, this slows a reader down by 7 per cent. As we have said earlier, anything you do as a writer which slows your readers down will also make them more likely to misunderstand what you are trying to tell them. In most typing pools these days, however, typists have been trained not to indent. The reason is that it makes typing marginally easier and faster and therefore cheaper. It is, though, simply transferring costs from one end of the communication line to the other. Mistakes at the readers' end could quite conceivably be much more expensive for an organisation. You will be helping to improve organisational communication if you can persuade your typists to indent the beginnings of paragraphs.

Similarly, following the guidance offered in Appendix 11.1, it is worth emphasising here that you will improve the process of communication if you can persuade your secretary or the typing pool supervisor to do one or all of the following. Choose a typeface which has serifs (the stands at the bottom of letters and the additional bits at the top of 'd', 'h', 'l' and so on). Avoid italic typefaces (which still exist in some older offices) as they are very difficult to read for any length of time. Try to avoid justifying lines (that is, having them all finish exactly at the right hand margin, as in books and newspapers). This text is not justified.

Choose a typeface which is at least the size of the common 'elite' typeface found on standard typewriters. Small typefaces (which can be produced by photographic reduction on to A5 paper) make for slow reading with all its pitfalls. Make sure that headings stand out (possibly by being in a different typeface from the text) and make sure that tables are clearly separated from the text.

Have your report typed in black on white paper. Avoid coloured papers if you can as most of these reduce the contrast between the print and the paper. This makes for more difficult reading. If you use a coloured cover, choose one which allows the black print to stand out clearly on it. As an example, black on white is read more than twice as fast as black on purple (which seems to be a popular choice of colour for covers – a sign of regal aspirations?).

7.6 Using Word Processors

For those as yet unfamiliar with word processors, they have six main components: the main computer, made up of a central processing unit, a random access memory (RAM) and a read only memory (ROM); the video screen; the keyboard; disk drives (usually for 5¼ inch or 8 inch floppy disks); the printer (preferably of 'letter quality, which produces printing of the same standard as an electric typewriter); and programs or software. If this is meaningless to you, you may find it worthwhile to read one of the many current books on word processing, or to ask a retailer for a demonstration.

Word processors offer the writer who has to produce a regular number of reports several facilities which are not otherwise easily available. Preparation material can be stored easily on disks. Material can be moved from one part of a report to another at will. Deletions and additions can be made easily. Layouts can be experimented with and changed. Reports can, in fact, be produced entirely by the manager himself without recourse to a typist. If he has a copier as well, he can produce multiple copies for distribution.

It is the ability to change anything you wish whenever you wish that is the key to the benefits a word processor can offer. Even a basic model is more versatile than the most sophisticated typewriter. A word processor can produce working copies of parts of a text at any time. When a writer has made all the changes he wants, he simply prints out a new, fresh copy.

Word processors will automatically centre words or titles. They will display on the video screen where the page breaks will be when a report is printed. They will automatically number pages. They will print bold face, which is useful for headings. They can be programmed to check for spelling mistakes and for some kinds of grammatical errors.

If your report has to go through several drafts before you are satisfied with it, a word processor abolishes the chore of re-typing. You simply press the appropriate keys and the new version is produced. Having reports on disks enables you to use parts of previous reports that are relevant to the current one without difficulty. This gives you considerable flexibility and also removes a degree of drudgery from reports which have common elements, like many visit reports or even feasibility reports (where all that is changed may be some of the statistical information).

The main advantages of word processors are, firstly, that change is effortless. Given a reasonable degree of skill in using a keyboard, adding to, taking away and moving around text is easy. Secondly, re-typing is unnecessary, the machine does it all. Thirdly, spelling can be checked automatically, as can grammatical correctness. Fourthly, word processors are quiet. You do not have to stay and listen to it print if you do not wish. If you have a word processor with a detachable keyboard, you are not chained to a desk, but can work anywhere in a room. Then again, unlike the conventional typewriter, the word processor automatically makes carriage returns. Research is easier because you can use data banks with the computer which forms the heart of the processor. Lastly, but by no means least, word processors are enjoyable to use. They can turn the chore of report writing into something resembling a pleasure. This, at the very least, may persuade you that a word processor would be worth the expense.

7.7 Exercises

So that you can assess how well you are able to put the instruction given in this section into practice, it will be useful to attempt at least one of the following exercises:

  (i) Select a report which you have written recently and apply the report analysis to it. Make a note of which questions you find most helpful. Do any questions appear not to be at all useful to you? Are there any questions which you would wish to add to the list?

 (ii) Apply each of the methods of assessing readability outlined in section 7.3 to a selection of your recent writing. What variations do you notice? Which method appears to meet your needs most closely?

(iii) If you are not a typist, obtain a simple self-instruction manual and the use of a typewriter for a week. See how much progress you can make in teaching yourself to type. At the end of the work, ask yourself whether you have made enough progress to encourage you to persevere. Compare the keyboards of a traditional typewriter and that to be found on a word processor. What similarities do you notice?

(iv) Obtain a selection of reports written by other people. Choose those that you think are particularly well written. What similarities and differences in layout and presentation do you notice? Can you identify any features which you feel it would be worth incorporating into your own reports?

7.8 Completion Checklist

At the end of this section you should be able to answer the following questions:

(i) Why is it necessary to carry out a report analysis in two parts?

(ii) On which two aspects of writing is the calculation for Gunning's Fog Index based?

(iii) What are the advantages of typing, as opposed to writing in longhand, the first draft of a report?

(iv) Why is an incubation period useful during the editing of a report?

(v) What are the main advantages of using a word processor during the report writing process?

8: Some Other Aspects of Report Writing

Writing a report may involve you in a number of other considerations. For instance, there may be certain legal implications arising from the statements you make; you may have a number of hidden objectives in writing a report. These and many other factors in the context within which you are writing may influence your approach to a report and its final outcome.

8.1 Legal Considerations

If you are in any doubt at all about whether something you have written contravenes a legal provision, you should seek expert legal advice.

The most obvious breaches of the law you are likely to be guilty of are those involving defamation and libel. You may also, if you have used any material which has already been published elsewhere, be guilty of infringing copyright (see section 8.4). Other possible breaches are those involving the Trade Descriptions Act, the Health and Safety at Work Act and the Sex Discrimination Act, especially in reports which are not clearly confidential. There are many others and hence the need for legal advice where any doubt exists.

8.2 Hidden Objectives

Sometimes you may have 'political' or hidden objectives when writing a report. Occasionally, you may not be aware of having such objectives. They can take many forms. You may wish to impress a superior with a good report. You may be trying to conceal some inconvenient information your researches have unearthed. You may try to present results in a better light than they deserve.

You may be trying to persuade customers to buy a product even though it will not meet their requirements as well as another. You may be wishing to cause trouble for a rival colleague or a competitor. You may be using a report to justify a previously determined position on an issue, problem or policy proposal.

The list is really endless and it is for your readers to detect the presence of hidden objectives rather than for you to have to reveal them. However, honesty is the best policy, or so it is said. Certainly, it makes for better communication if you can eliminate hidden objectives and be quite open and straightforward with your readers.

8.3 Security and Confidentiality

The Ministry of Defence has its own procedures for maintaining the security of the information which circulates within it. No commercial or public sector organisation should need to go to the same lengths. Where there is a need to secure information, there are some simple commonsense precautions which can be taken.

Limit the number of copies of the report for circulation. Number each copy and keep a record of who has received them. If necessary, recall all copies after sufficient time for everyone to have read it. Centralisation and close supervision of all copying facilities may be needed if an organisation produces many reports which must be kept confidential.

8.4 Copyright

As soon as something is written down, it is automatically copyrighted to the writer or, if he has produced it within working time or as part of his work, to the organisation. It may not be reproduced without permission.

There is normally no similar automatic copyright for information or ideas. The copyright is to the form of words used to express the material. Ideas can, however, be patented to restrict their exploitation by others.

You should have due regard to the copyright of others when writing your own reports. A short quotation may not need permission, but, as a rough guide, anything more than a couple of short paragraphs should not be included without the permission of the copyright holder. In most circumstances, this is unlikely to be refused. If you wish to quote extensively, there may be some form of agreed payment to be made.

When in doubt, seek permission. Under no circumstances quote at will without it. More and more individuals and organisations, perhaps because it is now so easy and so cheap to copy material, are becoming sensitive to breaches of copyright and are successfully suing in the courts for redress.

8.5 Reading Reports

Get into the habit of regularly reading the reports written by others. As you do so, read them critically. Look for points of merit as well as for faults. Pick out examples which are particularly good or particularly bad. This kind of systematic and analytical reading of the work of others will, over a period of time, bring about improvements and the avoidance of defects in your own writing.

It is also useful to do more general reading in order to stimulate your writing abilities. No one can tell you precisely how reading novels and non-fiction books on a wide range of subjects helps you become a better writer, but the fact remains that it does. Somehow or other contact with a variety of written material develops insights into the use of language and into expressing yourself clearly which cannot be taught in any other way. Reading what others have written is as important to a writer as studying other sportsmen and sportswomen is to athletes, soccer stars and golfers. A parallel in commercial terms would be studying the competition. You can always learn something from other people.

9: Problems in Writing Particular Kinds of Reports

Most of the advice given in preceding sections applies to most kinds of business, industrial and other reports. It will, however, be useful at this point to consider briefly some problems which may be peculiar to certain kinds of reports. In each case a possible solution to the problems is offered.

9.1 Visit Reports

Problems posed by visit reports include deciding what information is significant and what information is merely superfluous detail. Another problem is that each visit is in some respects unique and generates specific information to be processed. It is also often the case that the readership of visit reports is not easily definable.

The best solution would seem to be the provision of an 'open' pro forma with spaces for notes of conversations, problems found, advice given, and so on. Clear headings are necessary on the pro forma and a standard format for all the visits undertaken within an organisation is often possible. It may be necessary to make provision for cases where several visits have been made on a single trip.

9.2 Accident Reports

The fact that people's perceptions of events are unreliable is a problem here. There is often a failure to note essential points and an understandable preoccupation with any injured people rather than with the events which led up to the injuries. In addition, delay in completing the report can lead to inaccuracies.

What is needed is a 'closed' pro forma asking specific questions or requiring specific details. There should, however, be space for additional remarks or observations and for a diagram of the scene of the accident.

9.3 Inspection Reports

In these, it is necessary to cover a large number of items systematically. A further complication is that those who have to complete them may not be good at writing or at expressing themselves generally. There is usually a need to have the reports completed speedily.

Once again, a 'closed' pro forma is appropriate with a checklist of all the items to be covered. There should also be space for additional remarks, observations or recommendations for action.

9.4 Laboratory Reports

These reports need to show how the problem posed has been tackled. How conclusions have been reached must be made clear. One particular difficulty may be that those who prepare them may be specialists, though their readers may sometimes not be.

A clearly structured plan is needed with standardisation of expression where possible. Sometimes a kind of limited pro forma may be possible, with spaces for the insertion of results and larger spaces for more detailed exposition and description.

9.5 Sales Reports

These are somewhat trickier because inconvenient facts may be disguised or even omitted altogether. The language used may be 'coloured' or emotive. Sales figures may require interpretation for non-specialist readers.

The solution would seem to be broadly as for laboratory reports, but with a sales orientation in any standardised forms of expression which are possible.

9.6 Test Reports

Both problems and solutions here will be broadly similar to those suggested for inspection reports.

9.7 Technical Investigation Reports

Although these are usually longer and more detailed than either laboratory or inspection reports, many of the problems are similar. In particular, there can be the problem of the specialist who has to communicate with the non-specialist and must therefore choose his words carefully. It is essential to avoid jargon if this is the case.

The solution is to have a clearly structure plan with a checklist to ensure that all the necessary items have been covered. A special check should be made for unexplained terms which will cause the reader difficulty.

9.8 Management and Organisational Reports

Terms of reference may be difficult to specify in some reports. Preparation time may be inadequate. The readership may be wide and difficult to define.

Reports like this should be written following all the advice and techniques suggested in this guide. In this way, the problems should be easily overcome. If conclusions are likely to be sensitive, say, in reporting on the operation of a department, it can help to smooth the way if people affected are advised in advance.

9.9 Reports on People (Performance, Assessment, Reference)

The main problems here include uncertainty about what is significant information and what is irrelevant. When writing about other people, there is always the additional difficulty of finding exactly the right words to express one's thoughts. Here, perhaps more than in any other kinds of reports, a standardised approach is recommended.

One solution is to use a pro forma with a checklist. Rating scales can be useful in assessment and reference reports as they speed up completion when time may be short. There should, however, be additional space for remarks, observations and comments.

9.10 Reports on Meetings

These are different from minutes of meetings, where it is often sufficient simply to record the decisions made in the order they were taken. Reports on meetings may need to be prepared quickly. There may be difficulties over accuracy of interpretation of what actually took place. There is a need for some diplomacy in expression. There can be difficulties both in keeping up with the progress of the meeting while making notes and also playing an active part in the proceedings, and later in deciding how much detail to include.

The first decision to be made is whether in fact a report is required or simply minutes. An appropriate pattern of organisation should be selected (for example, either chronological or one based on the topics covered to give more prominence to the important issues discussed). The VULCAN system outlined in section 3.6 of this guide may be useful for taking notes during the meeting. The best approach may well be to follow the general advice and guidance given in this guide.

9.11 Project Reports

Numerous aspects may have to be related to each other. There may be more than one writer involved in the preparation of the report, requiring care to ensure consistency of style. Additionally, the total readership of the report may be unknown, which could make a proper readership analysis almost impossible to complete.

If several writers are involved, their first task is to agree on a plan. Each writer should be allocated complete sections and one person should be nominated as the editor; his task will be to ensure the necessary consistency. The advice given for 9.8 would be generally appropriate.

9.12 Feasibility Study Reports

These are very often carried out by experts for lay readers, with all the problems of suitable expression which that poses. There is the problem of how much detail to include. There may be a need to curtail length, although many readers of feasibility study reports may doubt that this is a consideration.

There should be a special emphasis on simplifying the structure and the language where possible. Facts will need to be clearly distinguished from opinions if lay readers are not to be misled. Again, the rest of the advice would be as for 9.8.

9.13 Survey Reports

Here, there is often an overwhelming amount of detail. Readers may not understand, or may not be sympathetic to, survey methods and therefore may be more than usually sceptical about the validity of the contents.

As much of the detailed information as possible should be put into appendices. It will also be important to pay special attention to justifying any conclusions which have been drawn. Again, the suggestions made in 9.8 would be relevant.

9.14 Other Research Reports

Once more, there is the problem of specialists writing for lay readers. The information to be conveyed may be more than usually complex. You will have to decide which are the best methods for presenting data.

Special emphasis should be given to simplicity of expression wherever the complexity of the information will allow this; jargon should be avoided. Visual aids in the form of graphs, charts and other illustrations and appendices will help keep the body of the report as uncluttered as possible. The rest of the advice would again be as for 9.8.

10: Conclusions and Recommendations

It will be necessary in most reports to extract the main conclusions and/or recommendations and re-state them in a separate section for emphasis. This is useful both for readers in a hurry and for those who wish to see quickly what other conclusions you have arrived at and what other recommendations you make in addition to the principal ones included in the summary.

As an example, the main recommendations in this guide are:

(i) You must know the purpose of the report and who will read it before you begin preparing for it.

(ii) You should set aside an incubation period between the preparation and planning stages for assessment.

(iii) You should plan the report carefully, using appropriate section headings.

(iv) You should write the report within as short a period of time as possible.

(v) You should follow the principles and techniques of effective writing as outlined in section 6.

(vi) You should keep your reports as short as possible.

(vii)You should keep the needs of your readers in mind at all times.

(viii)After you have written a report, you should carry out a detailed report analysis.

(ix)You should assess the readability of your report, using one of the formulae outlined in section 7.3

(x)You should submit reports on time, or earlier if possible.

In conclusion, it may be worth saying that if you do wish to improve your ability to write clearly and put into practice the advice and instruction offered in this guide, you will have made a useful contribution towards solving a few of the problems of business and industrial communication. You will have helped to increase both your own and your organisation's effectiveness.

11: Appendices

11.1 Readability of Written Materials – Some Notes

*"In the broadest sense, readability is the sum total
(including interactions) of all those elements within a given
piece of printed material that affects the success which a
group of readers have with it. The success is the extent to
which they understand it, read it at optimum speed and
find it interesting."*
E. Dale & J.S. Chall

Elements of Readability

1. Motivation – degree of interest shown by reader.

2. Perceptual Skill – efficiency of individual as a
    reader.

3. Language – degree of skill in expression of
    writer.

4. Language – degree of skill in understanding of
    reader.

5. Legibility – quality and appropriateness of type
    design, layout, etc.

6. Vocabulary – suitability of choice of words to
    readership.

7. Construction – pattern of organisation of
    material.

8. Aesthetic and Design Factors – appearance and
    attractiveness of materials, use of colour, etc.

9. Environmental Factors – lighting, temperature,
    noise, etc.

10. Eyesight – need for periodic checks.

Legibility – the Root of Readability

No reader can read effectively unless he can see the printed characters clearly. Some facts about legibility:

1. Some letters are easier to read than others:
   Letters of high legibility – d m p q w
   Letters of medium legibility – j r v x y
   Letters of low legibility – c e i n l

2. Factors in type design:
   Serifs (small embellishments to the basic shape of letters)
   Heaviness of stroke
   Emphasis of distinguishing characteristics
   Simplification of outline
   Emphasis of white space inside letter
   Width of letter

3. Italic type is more difficult to read than roman.

4. Lower case is easier to read than capitals. All capitals reduces speed.

5. Lines should not be justified.

6. Material is easiest to read at right angles to line of vision, 18 to 21 inches (about 50 cm) from eyes.

7. Matt paper is preferable to gloss paper.

8. Good contrast is needed between paper and print. *(See table on page 100).*

9. Illumination should be good, without glare, and come over shoulder from behind.

10. Upper half of print is more informative than lower half.

11. Right hand side of letters is more informative (when reading from left to right).

12. Ideally, lines should be 2 to 3½ inches (5 to 9 cm) in length.

13. 0.1 inch (2.5 mm) separation between columns is adequate.

14. Margins are unnecessary.

15. Type should not be smaller than 10 poi.: '72 points to the inch) in height.

16. Leading (space between lines) is probably unnecessary.

17. Indenting first line of paragraphs increases speed of reading.

18. Headings should stand out (e.g., by being in different typeface and by separating headings from text).

19. Tables should be distinguished from text.

20. Arabic numerals read faster than roman.

Effects of changing colour of paper and colour of print

Colour	Relative reading speed	Rank order of subjective legibility
Black on white	100.0	1
Green on white	97.0	4
Blue on white	96.6	2
Blue on yellow	96.2	3
Red on yellow	95.2	5
Red on white	91.1	6
Green on red	89.4	7
Orange on blue	86.5	8
Orange on white	79.1	9
Red on green	60.5	11
Black on purple	48.5	10

How to Make Written Materials Readable

1. Pay special attention to arousing and maintaining interest of reader.
2. Keep material as simple as complexity of information to be communicated allows. Aim for accuracy, brevity and clarity.
3. Check final presentation for legibility and readability.
4. Make materials attractive to look at and easy to handle.
5. Encourage provision of suitable environments for reading.

Sources
'Readability' by J. Gilliland, University of London Press, 1972.

'How to Make Type Readable' by D.G. Paterson &
M.A. Tinker, Harper, 1940.
'The Ergonomics of Journal Design' by E.C. Poulton &
Others, Applied Ergonomics, September 1970.
'Legibility of Print' by M.A. Tinker, University of
Minnesota Press, 1963.

11.2 Arrangement of Material for a Report

1.   Title Page – reports of more than about six pages.
2.   Summary (Synopsis or Abstract) – a summary of the entire report.
3.   Table of Contents – longer and more formal reports.
4.   Introduction – states the subject, indicates purpose and announces the plan of treatment.
5.   Preliminary Section – if there is more preliminary material than the introduction can reasonably hold or to provide for a fuller treatment of this material.
6.   Body of the Report – defines the nature of the investigation, the equipment used, the procedures followed, the detailed results obtained, and contains an analysis of results leading to conclusions and/or recommendations. Sectional headings.
7.   Conclusions and/or Recommendations – lists those essential points from the mass of detail which should be remembered. Reinforces conclusions drawn and recommendations made.
8.   Appendix/Appendices – separate potentially confusing detail from the body of the report.
9.   Bibliography – sources of information.
10. Covering letter – a polite gesture for formal reports, giving the authorisation for the report. Precedes the title page.

11.3 Oral Reports, Presentations and Briefings

Basically, there is little difference between a written report and an oral report (or presentation or briefing). What differences there are lie in the delivery of the report, rather than in the preceding stages. An oral report may be based on the same work and information as a written report.

An oral report should be planned in a similar way to a written report, being divided into three basic sections:

1. Introduction
2. Body of the Report
3. Conclusion

To put it simply, in the introduction tell the audience what you are going to speak about or show them, in the body of the report tell them accurately and logically all that you want to say about the subject, show them your charts, graphs and other aids, and in the conclusion summarise what you have said and shown, picking out the most important points for further emphasis and repetition.

The main difference between written and oral reports lies in the expression, that is the choice of words and the style of speech. In a written report, slang and colloquial expressions are completely inappropriate, but this is not always the case with oral reports. The best advice is talk to your audience in the manner which seems most natural and most likely to establish a favourable rapport. Unless this is done you will feel that you have not secured the full attention of your audience, and this is bound to affect your ability to put your ideas across effectively.

Oral reports or lectures should never simply be read. You should take notes on what you want to say, using similar headings to those you would use in a written report and use them as a guide. The real purpose of the notes is to prevent you forgetting any important part of your report, rather than to provide you with the actual words to use. No attempt should be made to memorise the report (this will make it sound unnatural, dull and uninteresting), though it does help if you can give a 'practice' talk beforehand when alone, or in the presence of a colleague who can be trusted to listen and possibly criticise constructively. This increases confidence.

Several other hints to successful speaking in public are:
1. Number the sheets of your notes clearly so that you do not confuse the order in which you want to say things. Have them typed if possible.
2. Speak distinctly, so that a person at the back of the room can hear clearly, but do not raise your voice too much.
3. If your mouth feels dry before you start, and there is no glass of water handy, relax your lower jaw, letting your lips scarcely touch each other, for a few moments. You will feel your mouth watering and the dryness will disappear. Alternatively, suck a fruit sweet or chew some gum before going in.
4. Remember the value of the pause in letting an important item of information sink in. Do not rush from statement to statement fearing that a pause indicates you have run dry. Never speak too quickly, and do not use long words if shorter ones will suit the purpose.
5. Use statistics carefully. Keep them to a minimum

as they seldom register when merely spoken. Put them in a hand-out or on a slide or overhead projector transparency and let them make a visual impact.

6. Avoid odd mannerisms and do not wander about restlessly, but move easily. Try not to fiddle with your notes or other objects.

7. Treat your audience as human beings. Talk *to* them rather than *at* them and do not address the wall at the back of the room. Maintain 'eye contact' with members of the audience.

These points may help a little, but the main points to remember in delivering an oral report, presentation or briefing, or speaking in public generally, are:

1. Know thoroughly what you are talking about.

2. Prepare your material carefully and speak with the aid of notes.

3. Practise what you are going to say at least once privately beforehand.

11.3.1 Listening

When listening to others presenting reports, or when listening during the preparation and information-gathering stage for any report, the following comments may be useful:

1. Make notes where appropriate (in some situations, it may be necessary or advisable to ask permission to do this).

2. Listen with a purpose and be aware of the speaker's objective.

3. Take an active part in conversations and discussions when possible.

4. When listening, give your whole attention to the speaker.

5. Be sensitive to information conveyed by tone of voice, choice of words, etc.
6. Try to grasp the overall pattern of organisation imposed by the speaker on his material.
7. Listen critically at all times, considering content, intentions and treatment, before making your evaluation.

12: Further Reading

The following books will be useful if you wish to spend further time on improving your report writing skills: An asterisk (*) indicates a book especially worth reading:

*Banks, R.A., 'Living English', Hodder & Stoughton, 1983.
Cooper, B., 'Technical Report Writing', Penguin, 1964.
*Damerst, W.A., 'Clear Technical Reports', Harcourt Brace Jovanovich, 1972.
Darbyshire, A.E., 'Report Writing', Edward Arnold, 1970.
Gallagher, W.J., 'Report Writing for Management', Addison-Wesley, 1969.
Houp. K.W. & Pearsall. T.E., 'Reporting Technical Information', Glencoe Press, 1969.
Harwell, G., 'Technical Communication', McGraw-Hill,
Lesikar, R.V., 'Report Writing for Business', Irwin, 1969.
*Mitchell, J., 'How to Write Reports', Fontana, 1974.
Shurter, R.L., Williamson, J.P. & Broehl, W.G., 'Business Research and Report Writing', McGraw-Hill, 1965.
*Sidney, E., 'Business Report Writing', Business Publications, 1965.
*Turk, C. & Kirkman, J., 'Effective Writing', Spon, 1982.
Turner, R.P., 'Technical Report Writing', Holt, Rinehart & Winston, 1971.

In addition to these, no one who has writing to do, whether at work or at home, should be without the following:

A good dictionary (such as The Penguin English Dictionary).

A thesaurus, or synonym finder (Roget's Thesaurus, published by Penguin, for example).

A grammar handbook (perhaps Partridge's 'Usage and Abusage', published by Penguin).

'The Complete Plain Words' by Sir Ernest Gowers, revised edition, Penguin 1987.